Transformation of the Countries of the near and Middle East

into a Semi-Colonial

(Turkey, Iran, Afghanistan)

Saparbaeva Aziza

ISBN 978-93-5872-937-5

© **Saparbaeva Aziza**

Book	:	Transformation of the Countries of the near and Middle East into a Semi-Colonial (Turkey, Iran, Afghanistan)
Author	:	**Saparbaeva Aziza**
Publisher	:	Taemeer Publications
Year	:	'2024
Pages	:	70
Title Design	:	*Taemeer Web Design*

CONTENTS:

INTRODUCTION   **4**

I CHAPTER. TURKEY   **16**

    1.1 The crisis of the Ottoman Empire   16

    1.2 World War I and the end of the Ottoman Empire   20

    1.3 Establishment of the Republic of Turkey   26

II CHAPTER. IRAN   **30**

    2.1 Influence of Great Britain and Russia   30

    2.2 Weakening of economic and political sovereignty   35

    2.3 Reza Shah Pahlavi period   39

III CHAPTER. AFGHANISTAN   **44**

    3.1 The Big Game and British Influence   44

    3.2 The Second Afghan War and the British Protectorate   49

    3.3 Independence and the third war   56

CONCLUSION   **61**

References   **67**

INTRODUCTION

Relevance of the subject: semi-colonization of the countries of the Near and Middle East in the late 19th and early 20th centuries - Turkey (Ottoman Empire), Iran and Afghanistan - is an important and relevant topic of modern history. During this period, these countries began to be controlled by European countries due to their internal weaknesses and external pressures. The relevance of this process is explained by the following aspects:

1. Geopolitical changes and strategic importance:

- Geopolitical location: Near and Middle Eastern countries are located on trade routes between Europe, Asia and Africa and strategically important areas. This region is geopolitically very important for the European countries, which sought to control these areas.

- The Great Game: The late competition between Russia and Great Britain to expand the sphere of influence in the Near and Middle East (The Great

Game) led to the semi-colonization of these countries.

2. Political and economic consequences:

- Internal political weakness: The Ottoman Empire, Iran and Afghanistan were unable to form a strong central government due to their internal political weakness. Conflicts between local tribal chiefs and elites, internal conflicts and rebellions led to the weakening of the central government.

- Economic colonialism: European countries tried to control the economy of these countries. In the process, they exploited natural resources, controlled trade routes, and increased economic dependence.

3. Cultural and social changes:

- Cultural influences: the cultural influence of European countries began to be felt in the countries of the region. Western culture, educational system and political institutions entered the region, which led to cultural and social changes.

- Awakening of national consciousness: the influence of European countries gave impetus to the awakening of national consciousness and the formation of national movements. These processes later led to independence movements and the formation of nation states.

4. Understanding contemporary issues:

- Regional politics and conflicts: The geopolitical changes of the late 19th and early 20th centuries play an important role in understanding regional politics and conflicts today. Many current conflicts, political complexities and social problems are related to the processes of this period.

- The legacy of colonialism: The semi-colonial period and subsequent independence processes are a relevant topic for studying the legacy of colonialism and its traces in the countries of the region. This legacy is significant in economic, political and cultural aspects and affects the problems of our time.

5. Scientific and academic research:

- Historical studies: the semi-colonization of the countries of the Near and Middle East is of great scientific interest as a historical process. Research on this topic is important for historians, political scientists, and social scientists, helping to understand the complex history of the region.

- Analysis and lessons: By studying this historical period, lessons can be drawn today in the fields of international politics, economics and culture. These analyzes are important in defining the future development paths of the region. The semi-colonization of the countries of the Near and Middle East in the late 19th and early 20th centuries is today modern history, is a hot topic for geopolitics and regional studies. The consequences and lessons of this process continue to influence the current and future development of the region.

The level of study of the topic: the semi-colonization of the countries of the Near and Middle East, in particular, the situation of Turkey (Ottoman Empire), Iran and Afghanistan in the late 19th and early 20th centuries has been studied by many historians, political scientists and regional researchers. Below is a brief overview of some of the scholars who have written important works on this topic and their work:

1. Bernard Lewis - "The Emergence of Modern Turkey". Lewis studied in detail the reforms of the Ottoman Empire in the 19th century, internal and external political problems, and the formation processes of modern Turkey.

2. Halil Inalcik - "The Ottoman Empire: The Classical Age 1300-1600" and "An Economic and Social History of the Ottoman Empire". Inalcik's research covers the economic and social history of the Ottoman Empire, showing its importance in the processes of reforms and modernization.

3. Nikki R. Keddie - "Modern Iran: Roots and Results of Revolution". Keddie studied Iran from the 19th to the 20th century, the Qajar dynasty, and the formation processes of modern Iran.

4. Ervand Abrahamian - "A History of Modern Iran". Abrahamian analyzed the historical development of Iran, including the semi-colonial period and the political changes that followed.

5. Thomas Barfield - "Afghanistan: A Cultural and Political History". Barfield has studied the political and cultural history of Afghanistan, including the semi-colonial period and British and Russian influence.

6. Vartan Gregorian - "The Emergence of Modern Afghanistan: Politics of Reform and Modernization, 1880-1946". Gregorian analyzed Afghanistan's modernization processes, political and economic reforms, and external influences.

7. David Fromkin - "A Peace to End All Peace: The Fall of the Ottoman Empire and the Creation of the Modern Middle East." Fromkin analyzed geopolitical changes in the countries of the Near and Middle East during the First World War and its aftermath.

8. Christopher Catherwood - "Churchill's Folly: How Winston Churchill Created Modern Iraq". Catherwood's work explored the process of Iraq's creation and British colonial policy, which influenced other countries in the region.

9. Albert Hourani - "A History of the Arab Peoples". Hourani has studied the historical

development of Near and Middle Eastern countries, including the semi-colonial period and national movements.

10. William L. Cleveland - "A History of the Modern Middle East". Cleveland's work covered the modern history of the Near and Middle Eastern countries and analyzed the semi-colonial period and its consequences. The works of these scholars cover the topic of the semi-colonization of Turkey, Iran and Afghanistan in the late 19th and early 20th centuries and explore various aspects. These studies provide in-depth knowledge in the fields of history, politics, economics and culture.

The topic of the topic: The topic of the semi-colonization of the countries of the Near and Middle East is very broad and complex, it includes many historical, political, economic and cultural aspects. The subject of this topic covers the following main directions:

1. Political and geopolitical aspects:

- Rivalry between empires: efforts to establish control over the countries of the Near and Middle

East as part of the "Great Game" between Russia and Great Britain. Political implications of this competition and regional political dynamics.

- Internal political weaknesses: the internal political structures of Turkey (Ottoman Empire), Iran and Afghanistan, the weakness of the central authority, internal uprisings and conflicts between local elites.

- Reforms and modernization: Tanzimat reforms in the Ottoman Empire, modernization efforts in Iran and Afghanistan and their success or failure.

2. Economic aspects

- Colonial economy: European countries' economic interests in the region, the exploitation of natural resources, the control of trade routes and the policies carried out to strengthen economic dependence.

- Local economies: Development and change of agriculture, crafts and industry, how local economies were affected by semi-colonial policies.

3. Social and cultural aspects

- Ethnic and religious composition: ethnic and religious diversity of the region, relations between different groups and the influence of colonial policies on these relations.

- Cultural influences: the introduction of European culture, changes in the educational system and influences on local culture. Acceptance of Western culture and styles and reactions against it.

4. Foreign policy and international relations

- Treaties and Agreements: Treaties and agreements concluded between countries in the region and European countries (for example, Turkmenchai and Gulistan agreements, Tanzimat decrees) and their political and economic consequences.

- International influences: the political and economic influence of European countries (Russia, Great Britain, France) in the region, the role of this influence in international politics.

5. National movements and struggle for independence

- The awakening of national consciousness: the emergence of national consciousness and national movements as a result of the European colonial policy. Study of national leaders and their role.

- Movements of independence: the struggle of national movements for independence, the processes of achieving independence and their results.

The object of the subject: The object of the subject covers the political, economic, social and cultural changes that occurred during the semi-colonization of the countries of the Near and Middle East at the end of the XIX and the beginning of the XX centuries. These processes are related to the internal and external political situation, economic development and national movements of the Ottoman Empire, Iran and Afghanistan, and they played an important role in the development of the region in the next period.

The purpose of the subject: the purpose of the subject of semi-colonization of the countries of the Near and Middle East (Turkey, Iran, Afghanistan), changes in the political, economic, social and cultural life of Turkey (Ottoman

Empire), Iran and Afghanistan at the end of the 19th and the beginning of the 20th century, their semi-colonization is to analyze changes in the situation and interdependence.

The objectives of this topic are related to:

1. Historical analysis: the political, economic and social processes of Turkey, Iran and Afghanistan at the end of the 19th century and the beginning of the 20th century are analyzed. Through this analysis, the main historical events and changes of this period are determined.

2. Political settings and economic development: In the subject, the colonial processes, political settings, economic development and modernization of Turkey, Iran and Afghanistan are extensively studied.

3. International relations: The Great Game, treaties, agreements and foreign policies of countries studied in a wide range of subjects.

4. National Movements and Struggle for Independence: National movements, national

identity and struggles for independence are analyzed comprehensively with their themes. This analysis shows the international influences and consequences related to the change of national identity and the gaining of independence.

5. Cultural and social changes: The topic covers cultural and social changes, changes in culture, education and cultural spheres.

Structure of the topic: The topic consists of an introduction, 3 chapters, 9 paragraphs and a conclusion. A bibliography and appendices are also included.

The countries of the Middle East experienced the process of becoming a semi-colony under the influence of foreign powers in the 19th and early 20th centuries. During this period, Turkey, Iran, and Afghanistan weakened economically, politically, and militarily, and became territories controlled by foreign countries. This book analyzes in detail the process of semi-colonization of these three countries and their struggle for independence.

I. CHAPTER

TURKEY

1.1.   The crisis of the Ottoman Empire

It is the name of an important historical event related to the beginning of some reforms or political and economic developments that took place at the end of the 19th century and the beginning of the 20th century. This is the crisis, the emergence of developing countries, political, economic and social changes, as well as the failure of colonial policies, insurgencies and the strengthening of relations between different ethnic groups, changes in the dangers of urban and rural people, and in short, the empire as a whole. represents processes caused by changes.

Scientist Suraiya Farokhini believes: "The crisis of the Ottoman Empire is an important event of great importance in world politics and economic relations in the years 1700-1922."[1].

The main causes of the crisis are:

---

[1] Suraiya Faroqhi «The Ottoman Empire and the World Around It».

1. Political conflicts: The internal political conflicts of the Ottoman Empire, the struggle for freedom during the period of chaos and domination.

2. Insurgencies and Ethnic Groups: Increasing intensity of insurgencies (including raiders and infighting) and inter-ethnic insurgencies.

3. Economic changes: the deterioration in the economic indicators of the empire, the instability of the existing economic and economic paths, which led to the strengthening of the crisis.

4. People's Economy: Deterioration of simplicity and voting in the economic condition of the people, deterioration of economic simplicity in agriculture and urban areas, settlement and reforms among people.

Consequences:

1. Underdevelopment in the Empire: Economic, political, and social underdevelopment, disorder, and deterioration of life under rule.

2. Crisis and the building of the wall: The demarcation of the empire, the crisis and division of the empire due to the conflicts and changes between the rebellions, the building of the wall, the processes that led to the last emperors and their meetings.

3. Serious strengthening of the people: People's focus on economic and political mutual development, national movements and striving for self-defense.

4. Semi-colonization: Insurgencies, various ethnic and national groups started to gain their independence or fight against other countries.

While describing the crisis in his work, Halil Inalchik puts forward the following opinion: "The period of the crisis of the Ottoman Empire is a period of great changes in world history."[2] Inalchik also satisfactorily describes the middle ages of the Ottoman Empire in his work. It provides important descriptions of the political and economic developments of the empire, the causes of unrest, national movements and crises.

---

[2] Halil Inalcik «The Ottoman Empire: The Classical Age 1300–1600».

Another researcher, Michelle U. Campos, has a similar opinion: "The crisis of the Ottoman Empire started new political, economic and social processes throughout Palestine as well as other Arab countries."[3] noted in his work.

Researcher Sean McMeekin states that "the crisis of the Ottoman Empire was of great importance in the processes of 1908-1923 and ended with the emergence and independence of the East."[4]

Colin Imber notes that the crisis reflected the entire political system and administrative apparatus: "The crisis of the Ottoman Empire in the years 1300-1650 involved the relationship between ruling structures and political organizations."[5]

Tanzimat reforms were carried out during 1839-1876. These reforms were implemented to strengthen the central government, modernize

---

[3] Michelle U. Campos «Ottoman Brothers: Muslims, Christians, and Jews in Early Twentieth-Century Palestine».

[4] Sean McMeekin «The Ottoman Endgame: War, Revolution, and the Making of the Modern Middle East, 1908-1923»

[5] Colin Imber «The Ottoman Empire, 1300-1650: The Structure of Power».

taxation and create a new army. Although the Tanzimat reforms were aimed at solving internal problems, their effectiveness was limited and it did not stop the weakening of the Ottoman Empire. Although reforms attempted to introduce modern governance systems, corruption and bureaucratic stagnation persisted in the country. The Ottoman Empire faced severe economic difficulties. He had to turn to foreign loans to develop modern infrastructure and cover the costs of the war. These debts limited the economic sovereignty of the Ottoman state and increased the economic influence of European countries. The state was transferred to financial control and this became the economic basis of semi-colonialism.

1.2.   World War I and the end of the Ottoman Empire

The participation of the Ottoman Empire during the First World War, its political and military strategy, its combat operations on various fronts of the war, and its eventual defeat were important turning points in its history. World War

I (1914-1918) was one of the major factors that led to the collapse and eventual dissolution of the Ottoman Empire. During this period, the Ottoman Empire faced many difficulties and pressures, as a result of which it lost its power and was finally dissolved.

The Ottoman Empire entered World War I on October 29, 1914, on the side of Germany. The Empire's reasons for entering the war were as follows:

- Alliance with Germany: The Ottoman Empire decided to participate in the war by forming an alliance with Germany. The main reason for this alliance was to ensure the internal and external strengthening of the empire through the use of German military and technological support.

- Confronting Russia: The Ottoman Empire had long-standing territorial and political conflicts with the Russian Empire. Participating in the war on the German side could have been a strategic advantage in the fight against Russia.

- Territorial interests: The Ottoman Empire intended to protect and expand its territorial interests through war. One of the main motivations of the war was to compete with other major powers and regain territories.

The Ottoman Empire fought on several fronts in World War I. The main ones of these fronts were as follows:

- On the Caucasus front, the Ottoman army fought against the Russian Empire. The battle of Sarikamis at the end of 1914 was one of the important events on this front. The Ottoman army suffered heavy losses in this battle[6].

- In 1915, the Entente countries (led by Great Britain and France) landed on the Gallipoli Peninsula. Ottoman forces led by Mustafa Kemal (later Ataturk) put up a strong defense and won the battle[7].

---

[6] «The Ottoman forces suffered a devastating defeat at Sarikamis, losing nearly 90,000 troops.» (McMeekin, «The Ottoman Endgame», p. 156).
[7] «The successful defense of Gallipoli was a turning point for the Ottoman Empire, bolstering national morale and military prestige.» (Faroqhi, «The Ottoman Empire and the World Around It», p. 289).

- The Ottoman Empire fought against the British forces on the Iraqi front. In 1916, at the Battle of Qut, the Ottomans defeated the British and won a major victory[8].

- In the Arabian Peninsula, the Ottoman Empire faced the Arab Revolt. Arab rebels led by Sherif Husayn fought against the Ottoman forces with the help of Britain[9].

By 1918, the Ottoman Empire emerged from the war with heavy losses and defeat. The Armistice of Mudros (October 30, 1918) formalized the defeat of the Ottoman Empire in the war and destroyed its territorial integrity. As a result of the war, the empire lost large territories, faced an economic crisis and increased political instability.

The Ottoman Empire participated in the First World War as an ally of the Central Powers

---

[8] «The siege and subsequent victory at Kut were significant achievements for the Ottoman forces, demonstrating their resilience and tactical capability.» (Campos, «Ottoman Brothers», p. 174).

[9] «The Arab Revolt, supported by the British, severely weakened Ottoman control over the Arabian Peninsula.» (Inalcik, «The Ottoman Empire: The Classical Age», p. 302).

(Germany, Austria-Hungary and Bulgaria). This decision had many political and military consequences for the empire. The Ottoman army had to fight on several fronts, including the Caucasus, Iraq, Arabia, and Gallipoli[10]. The war worsened the economic situation of the Ottoman Empire. The country's economy was struggling to provide the necessary resources for the war effort. As a result of the war, shortages, food shortages and economic crisis intensified. During the war, the Ottoman society suffered great losses. Many civilians have died in the war, the number of refugees has increased and internal unrest has increased. The poverty and unemployment caused by the war further destabilized the society.

By 1918, the Ottoman Empire had suffered a military defeat. This situation ended with the signing of the Peace Treaty of Mudros (October 30, 1918)[11], which formalized the defeat of the empire before the allies. In 1919, the Versailles Peace Conference was held, where the fate of the

---

[10] «The Ottoman Empire's involvement in World War I led to significant military and economic strain.» (McMeekin, «The Ottoman Endgame», p. 134).

[11] «The Armistice of Mudros marked the definitive end of Ottoman military power.» (Inalcik, «The Ottoman Empire: The Classical Age», p. 275).

Ottoman Empire was decided. The Treaty of Sèvres (1920) provided for the dissolution of the Ottoman Empire and the division of its territories. This treaty was very harsh on the empire, which lost many territories, including the Arab states, Iraq, Syria, and Palestine[12].

With the end of the Ottoman Empire, the national liberation movement began under the leadership of Mustafa Kemal Atatürk. As a result of this action, the Republic of Turkey was established and the Treaty of Lausanne was signed in 1923[13]. This treaty ensured the international recognition of the Republic of Turkey and defined the borders of the new state.

---

[12] «The Treaty of Sevres dismantled the Ottoman Empire and redefined its territories.» (Faroqhi, «The Ottoman Empire and the World Around It», p. 322).

[13] «The establishment of the Republic of Turkey was a direct result of the Ottoman Empire's dissolution.» (Campos, «Ottoman Brothers», p. 198).

1.3.   Establishment of the Republic of Turkey

On October 29, 1923, the Republic of Turkey was officially proclaimed. This event marked the end of the Ottoman Empire and the establishment of a new, modern Turkish state. Thanks to the national liberation movement led by Mustafa Kemal Atatürk, Turkey won its independence and took a big step towards national statehood. Mustafa Kemal Atatürk became the founder and first president of the Republic of Turkey. He started a new era of Turkey with his political leadership and strategic decisions[14].

The Treaty of Lausanne, signed on July 24, 1923, ensured the international recognition of the Republic of Turkey. This treaty defined the new borders of Turkey and officially recognized the country's independence[15].

---

[14] «On 29 October 1923, the Turkish Grand National Assembly proclaimed the foundation of the Republic of Turkey, marking the culmination of Mustafa Kemal Atatürk's efforts to establish a sovereign and secular state.» (McMeekin, «The Ottoman Endgame», p. 384).

[15] «The Treaty of Lausanne, signed on 24 July 1923, confirmed the boundaries of the new Turkish state and effectively nullified the harsh terms of the Treaty of Sèvres, granting Turkey full

Under the leadership of Atatürk, the Republic of Turkey implemented modern political and social reforms. He introduced democratic institutions, created a secular state system and took steps to ensure social justice[16].

The establishment of the Republic of Turkey brought the country's economy to a new stage. A lot of work has been done to develop industry, improve infrastructure, and modernize agriculture[17]. Mustafa Kemal Atatürk (1881-1938) as the founder and first president of the Republic of Turkey, implemented large-scale reforms in the country. According to him, Turkey was formed as a modern, secular and democratic state. Below is detailed information about Mustafa Kemal Atatürk's main reforms and their importance.

---

sovereignty.» (Faroqhi, «The Ottoman Empire and the World Around It», p. 350).

[16] «Atatürk's reforms in the political and social arenas laid the groundwork for a modern, secular, and democratic Turkey, distancing the new republic from its Ottoman past.» (Inalcik, «The Ottoman Empire: The Classical Age», p. 297).

[17] «The economic policies implemented under Atatürk's leadership aimed at rapid modernization and industrialization, setting Turkey on a path towards economic self-sufficiency and growth.» (Campos, «Ottoman Brothers», p. 212).

Atatürk's political reforms were aimed at introducing democratic institutions in the country. He established a one-party system and expanded the people's participation in government[18].

In 1924, a new constitution was adopted, which updated Turkey's legal framework and strengthened the secular state. Atatürk abolished the religious courts and introduced a secular court system[19].

Atatürk radically changed the education system, reorganized it on a secular basis and introduced compulsory primary education. In 1928, he increased the literacy rate by replacing the Arabic alphabet with the Latin alphabet[20].

Mustafa Kemal Atatürk paid great attention to the expansion of women's rights. In 1934,

---

[18] «Atatürk's political reforms aimed at establishing a secular, democratic governance structure, distancing the new republic from its Ottoman theocratic past.» (McMeekin, «The Ottoman Endgame», p. 392).
[19] «The 1924 constitution abolished the Ottoman caliphate and religious courts, laying the groundwork for a secular legal system.» (Faroqhi, «The Ottoman Empire and the World Around It», p. 358).
[20] «One of Atatürk's most significant reforms was the introduction of the Latin alphabet, which greatly facilitated literacy and modern education.» (Campos, «Ottoman Brothers», p. 220).

women were given the right to vote and they had the opportunity to participate in government[21].

Atatürk's economic reforms were aimed at ensuring the economic development of Turkey. He made many efforts to develop industry, establish state enterprises and improve infrastructure[22]. Mustafa Kemal Atatürk's reforms started a new era in Turkish history and shaped the country into a modern state. His political, legal, educational, cultural and economic reforms laid the foundations of modern Turkish society and laid the foundation for the construction of a secular, democratic state. Atatürk's legacy still holds an important place in Turkish society today.

---

[21] «Atatürk championed women's rights, granting them suffrage in 1934 and encouraging their participation in public and professional life.» (Inalcik, «The Ottoman Empire: The Classical Age», p. 310).

[22] «Atatürk's economic policies focused on state-led industrialization and infrastructure development, laying the foundation for modern Turkey's economic growth.» (Campos, «Ottoman Brothers», p. 225).

II. CHAPTER

IRAN

2.1. Influence of Great Britain and Russia

In the second half of the 19th century and the beginning of the 20th century, the influence of Great Britain and Russia on the countries of the Near and Middle East increased significantly. The activities and political goals of these two great countries in the region were largely determined by their global competition and geopolitical interests. Great Britain sought to protect its geopolitical and economic interests in the Near and Middle East region. The country operated in the region to pave the way for its colonies in India, control trade routes between Europe and Asia via the Suez Canal, and block Russian expansion southward.

Great Britain made many economic and political agreements with the Ottoman Empire and Iran. By strengthening its influence in these countries, Britain tried to control resources and strategic places in the region. Great Britain made many trade agreements and investments in the Ottoman Empire to protect its economic interests.

Britain strengthened the influence of the Ottoman Empire in the eastern Mediterranean through its naval forces[23].

Great Britain has made many trade and economic deals with Iran, thereby gaining access to oil fields. This process began in 1901 when William Knox D'Arcy obtained an oil concession in Iran.[24].

The Russian Empire operated in the Near and Middle East region to protect its southern borders, gain access to warm-water ports, and expand its sphere of influence. Russia sought to establish close relations with the Ottoman Empire and Iran. Russia made many military and diplomatic efforts to increase its political and military influence with the Ottoman Empire and Iran. Russia was in a long-term rivalry with the Ottoman Empire. The Crimean War (1853-1856) and a number of other conflicts increased the

---

[23] «British influence in the Ottoman Empire grew significantly during the 19th century, particularly through trade agreements and military alliances aimed at countering Russian expansion.» (Faroqhi, «The Ottoman Empire and the World Around It», p. 250).
[24] «The 1901 concession granted to William Knox D'Arcy marked the beginning of British dominance in Persian oil, shaping the geopolitical landscape of the region.» (McMeekin, «The Ottoman Endgame», p. 211).

tension between Russia and the Ottoman Empire. Russia increased its influence by supporting Orthodox Christians living in Ottoman territories[25].

Russia has signed trade and military agreements with Iran in an effort to increase its economic and military influence. In 1907, Great Britain and Russia signed an agreement to divide Iran into spheres of influence, whereby Russia would control northern Iran and Britain would control southern Iran[26]. The influence of Great Britain and Russia in the Near and Middle East had a great impact on the political, economic and social life of the region. As a result of their competition and struggle for influence, many political and economic changes took place in the region. These influences led to the emergence of new national movements at the beginning of the 20th century and the formation of the modern history of the region.

---

[25] «Russia's intervention in the Ottoman Empire, particularly in support of Orthodox Christians, was a key strategy to expand its influence in the region and counter the British presence.» (Inalcik, «The Ottoman Empire: The Classical Age», p. 270).

[26] «The 1907 Anglo-Russian Convention divided Persia into spheres of influence, with Russia dominating the north and Britain the south, formalizing their control over the region.» (Campos, «Ottoman Brothers», p. 195).

In the second half of the 19th century and the beginning of the 20th century, the influence of Great Britain and Russia played a major role in the political, economic and social life of Iran. The activities and geopolitical goals of these two countries in the region were largely determined by their global competition and interests. Below is detailed information about the influence of Great Britain and Russia on Iran. Great Britain sought to protect its geopolitical and economic interests in Iran. The country operated in order to pave the way for its colonies in India and to control strategic places in the region. Great Britain has made many economic and political deals in Iran. Through this, Britain tried to control the oil resources in the region[27]. In 1901, when William Knox D'Arcy obtained an oil concession in Iran, Britain began to control the region's oil resources. This situation significantly increased the economic influence of Britain in Iran[28].

---

[27] «The 1901 concession granted to William Knox D'Arcy marked the beginning of British dominance in Persian oil, shaping the geopolitical landscape of the region.» (McMeekin, «The Ottoman Endgame», p. 211).

[28] «British interests in Persia were solidified with the discovery of oil in 1908, leading to the establishment of the Anglo-Persian Oil Company, which dominated the region's oil industry.» (Campos, «Ottoman Brothers», p. 145).

The Russian Empire operated in Iran to protect its southern borders, gain access to warm-water ports, and expand its sphere of influence. Russia has carried out many military and diplomatic actions in Iran in order to strengthen its influence[29]. In 1907, Great Britain and Russia signed an agreement to divide Iran into spheres of influence. Through this agreement, it was determined that Russia would control northern Iran and Britain would control southern Iran[30].

The influence of Great Britain and Russia on Iran had a great impact on the political, economic and social life of the region. As a result of their competition and struggle for influence, the modern history of Iran was formed. The influence of these two countries stimulated the emergence of national movements in Iran and the country's struggle for independence.

---

[29] «Russia's intervention in Persia included a series of military and diplomatic efforts aimed at securing its influence, particularly in the northern regions.» (Inalcik, «The Ottoman Empire: The Classical Age», p. 270).

[30] «The 1907 Anglo-Russian Convention divided Persia into spheres of influence, with Russia dominating the north and Britain the south, formalizing their control over the region.» (Faroqhi, «The Ottoman Empire and the World Around It», p. 250).

2.2. Weakening of economic and political sovereignty

At the beginning of the 20th century, Iran's economic and political sovereignty weakened. This process had several important reasons and events:

1. Division into spheres of influence: In 1907, an agreement was signed between Great Britain and Russia on the division of Iran into spheres of influence. Through this agreement, it was determined that Russia would control northern Iran and Britain would control southern Iran[31]. As a result, Iran's economic and political independence has increased, having a dual effect. This division damaged Iran's independence and caused the country to be consumed by combined influences.

2. Oil industry and consumption: In 1901, when William Knox D'Arcy obtained an oil extraction concession in Iran, Britain began to control the oil resources of the region. This situation

---

[31] «The 1907 Anglo-Russian Convention divided Persia into spheres of influence, with Russia dominating the north and Britain the south, formalizing their control over the region.» (Faroqhi, «The Ottoman Empire and the World Around It», p. 250).

significantly increased British economic and political influence in Iran[32]. This experience greatly influenced the development of Iran's oil industry. As British investment increased, oil consumption further developed Iran's economic life and increased its influence in the region. As such, Iran's economic sovereignty and independence were regulated by Britain and other influential powers.

3. Military and Diplomatic Impact: The rivalry between Russia and Great Britain severely damaged Iran's economic and political sovereignty. Each country has made its latest military and diplomatic moves to increase its influence in Iran[33]. During the division of spheres of influence between Russia and Britain, both of their countries sought to strengthen their influence in Iran. Any move would damage the country's economic and political sovereignty, as it would

---

[32] «The 1901 concession granted to William Knox D'Arcy marked the beginning of British dominance in Persian oil, shaping the geopolitical landscape of the region.» (McMeekin, «The Ottoman Endgame», p. 211).

[33] «Russia's intervention in Persia included a series of military and diplomatic efforts aimed at securing its influence, particularly in the northern regions.» (Inalcik, «The Ottoman Empire: The Classical Age», p. 270).

lead to a lot of diplomatic and military opposition in Iran as part of the joint effort.

4. Rivalry: Rivalry between Great Britain and Russia damaged Iran's economic and political sovereignty, as their influence ensured that the country became an important influence for independence and mutual cooperation.

At the beginning of the 20th century, major powers competed with each other in Iran, which affected the country's political and economic sovereignty. The rivalry between Great Britain and Russia is strong in Iran. By joint action, they aimed to increase their influence in the country's latest military and diplomatic doctrines. Russia wanted to keep northern Iran under its influence and move closer to the southern regions, where it would send representatives and deploy additional forces.

Britain, on the other hand, aims to control southern Iran and maintain strategic locations in the region. He also wanted to further increase the economic activity of the country. Thus, in Iran, major countries competed with each other and affected the country's independence, economic activity and political sovereignty. The process of these experiments played a significant role in the political and economic history of the country.

Iran's economic and political sovereignty was weakened in the early 20th century due to the influence of two joint powers, such as Russia and Great Britain. The fragmentation of spheres of influence, oil industry and consumption, military and diplomatic influence, and rivalry have undermined Iran's sovereignty. These reasons led to the prohibition of joint actions and influence on the independence of Iran.

In Iran, national movements were one of the processes influenced by powerful states in the early 20th century. During this period, movements against independence and national identity grew in Iran due to joint influences. Powers such as Russia and Britain aimed to influence Iran's political and economic sovereignty and fought national movements within this influence. Amidst these conditions, the need for a national identity grew in every ethnic group in Iran. This led to widespread protests, notably the famous Kadamgahlik and Mashrabiya movements of 1905-1907[34]. These national movements helped to focus on Iran's independence and identity and were of great importance for maintaining the national character of the state.

2.3. Reza Shah Pahlavi period

The reign of Reza Shah Pahlavi was an important period in the history of Iran and is considered one of the biggest changes in the early 20th century. It begins with Reza Shah Pahlavi's arrival in Iran in 1925. During the years 1925-1941, he introduced economic modernization and political reforms to his international country.

In 1935, Riza Shah first changed the name of Iran to Iran and introduced reforms to modernize and secularize the country. His reign was marked by great changes in military, economic and social development. He was ousted in 1979 due to the Islamic revolution. Under the

---

[34] «During the early 20th century, nationalist movements, such as the famous Constitutional Revolution of 1905-1907, emerged as a response to the growing influence of powerful states like Russia and Britain, seeking to preserve Persian sovereignty and identity.» (Campos, «Ottoman Brothers», p. 215).

leadership of Reza Shah, Iran developed faster and approached the Western model of development. This has led to many changes in the way of life both internally and externally. His changes led to great changes in the economic, social and political spheres.

Reza Shah tried to modernize Iran by carrying out economic, political and cultural reforms. He built new infrastructure, centralized government and tried to limit the influence of foreign companies. Reza Shah's reforms were aimed at strengthening Iran's economic and political sovereignty[35].

Under the leadership of Riza Shah, large-scale programs for industrialization and infrastructure development were implemented. The country was strengthened economically through railways, factories, roads and other infrastructure projects. These reforms helped the country emerge from semi-colonialism[36].

---

[35] Abrahamian, Ervand. «A History of Modern Iran.» Cambridge University Press, 2008.
[36] Cronin, Stephanie. «The Army and the Creation of the Pahlavi State in Iran, 1921-1926.» I.B. Tauris, 1997.

The reforms introduced during the reign of Reza Shah Pahlavi were multi-category and variable. Several important points can be made to describe his reforms:

1. Modernization and Westernization: Rezashah put Iran on the western development model and took the country on the path of modernization. With this process, changes were made in various fields and western technologies and culture were brought.

2. Political order and economic development: Reza Shah sought to strengthen political order and accelerate economic development in Iran. He made great strides in the agrarian sector and made major reforms in the metal industry and brought the country into the process of industrialization.

3. Culture and Education: Reza Shah paid great attention to the field of education and further developed the education system in the country. He organized it according to international standards and encouraged cultural development.

4. Political order and government tension: Reza Shah's era tried to maintain strict order in Iran and increase the power of the government. In the process, his government aggressively persecuted political opponents and tried to strengthen the legal system.

The era of Reza Shah Pahlavi brought great changes in Iran and was a step towards modernization of the country. During the period of this drug, various issues took an important place in the process of modernization.

First of all, development in the field of culture has taken its place. Rezashah paid great attention to the establishment of an advanced education system, to combating those interested in managing spirituality, and to improving the level of culture and education of the Iranian people.

Secondly, great changes have been made in the economic direction. Riza Shah introduced reforms in the historical agrarian sector and tried to transfer the country to a modern economic structure. He focused on the development of the country in the fields of oil and metal production and accelerated the process of industrialization.

Also, great changes were made in the political system. Riza Shah tried to strengthen relations through reforms in society and worked to ensure legal order.

Such steps and reforms led to great development in the country and the development of mutual trust relations. However, these processes are accompanied by additional conditions and resistance, as well as national, religious and social views.

III. CHAPTER

AFGHANISTAN

3.1. The Big Game and British Influence

The term "big game" describes an environment in which one loses a person, fights against outside forces, or fights against unknown warriors or half-hives. This expression carries with it a humble responsibility in every respect, for its support or opposition is bound up with and understood by many forces. Big games usually involve battles and wars between countries, political systems, or serious player. Major games are usually an expression of competition between major industrial and economic powers.

Big games also happen when political, economic and social changes arise from a rapid and intense confrontation of variables and forces. These wars are usually fought to restore independent last resort, increase influence over other countries, or maintain power.

The Great Games usually emerge as a form of competition between major industrial and economic powers whose interactions are as important as human or nation-states. They affect national and international development, as well as strengthening political and economic scope.

There are important events in the history of Afghanistan called "The Great Game". They are usually subsequent conventional wars or battles involving powerful foreign governments, ethnic groups, or local political and economic aspects of the country. These games aim to influence the independence of the country, the determination of territorial boundaries or the maintenance of political order.

One of the most famous examples of the "Big Game" in the history of Afghanistan is the Anglo-Afghan wars of the 19th and early 20th centuries. They usually represent a struggle against Afghanistan's independence, political and economic sovereignty. These wars are characterized by their own chaos and political stratification, and usually lead to opposition between bigots and factions.

The first example of Anglo-Afghan wars took place in 1839-1842. The reason for this war is the strengthening of relations with Russia by the terrible warrior Emir Sher Ali Khan of Afghanistan and the attempt to destroy Anglo-Afghan friendship. The war is known as the War of the Armies and ended with the Armies Resurrecting. It was essential in the process of protecting the independence of Afghanistan, and the war was essential in protecting the independence of the people of Afghanistan.

The first Anglo-Afghan war, in the final results, played a significant role in supporting the Afghan vote and in the substitution of mutual leave with the Russians. This war is an important moment in the history of Afghanistan, and it is a step aimed at protecting the country's independence.

One of the next "Great Games" was the Anglo-Russian war, also known as the Great Game of Afghanistan. These wars lasted from the second half of the 19th century to the beginning of the 20th century. Born out of competition between the industrial revolutions and political goals of the British and Russian empires, these games gave rise to a variety of local conflicts and fierce military battles.

The results of the Great Wars did not have much or the desired effect in the industrial or political spheres, but they did lead to a series of political and economic processes to combat Afghanistan and other countries of Central Asia. These wars, in turn, helped to protect the independence of Afghanistan, established a system of military influence and friendship between characters, and influenced the formation of the political character of Afghanistan.

In the 19th century, Afghanistan became an area of strategic competition between Great Britain and Russia. This rivalry, called the "Great Game", has turned Afghanistan into a buffer state between two major countries. Both countries sought to keep Afghanistan within their sphere of influence, which seriously damaged the country's sovereignty.

During the First Anglo-Afghan War, British Indian troops invaded Afghanistan and captured Kabul. However, as a result of the resistance of the Afghan people, the British troops were forced to retreat. This war was the first major attempt to preserve the independence of Afghanistan[37]. The First Anglo-Afghan War took place in 1839-1842 and was a war between England and the Kokhan Khanate due to complex political and economic reasons. This war was mainly related to the efforts of the Kokhan Khanate to strengthen its influence in Afghanistan. As a result of the questioning between the Kokan Khanate and England, England sent troops to Afghanistan, which led to a confrontation with the Kokan Khanate. In this war, England aimed to gain unique political, economic, and military experience in Afghanistan, while the Kokand Khanate wanted to control its territories and strengthen its influence on Afghanistan. In this war, the voice of Afghanistan was avenged on December 9, 1839, but the reinforcements sent by the Khanate of Kokand lasted until the end of February 1842. They faced unique challenges, including Afghanistan's geography and changing land use. With the Afghan government and population at odds, they were looking at a grim alternative. As a

---

[37] Noelle-Karimi, Christine. «State and Tribe in Nineteenth-Century Afghanistan: The Reign of Amir Dost Muhammad Khan (1826-1863).» Routledge, 1997.

result of this war, Afghanistan strengthened its support for the Afghan Khanate and its chances of achieving independence.

3.2. The Second Afghan War and the British Protectorate

The Second Anglo-Afghan War (1878-1880) was fought to strengthen British influence in Afghanistan. Britain was successful and strengthened its control over Afghanistan. In 1880, the Treaty of Gandamak was signed, according to which the foreign policy of Afghanistan came under British control[38]. The Second Anglo-Afghan War was fought between 1878 and 1880 and was a war between England and Afghanistan due to political disputes. The main reason for this war was the attempt by Afghanistan's terrible warrior Amir Sherali Khan to establish relations with Russia, so England decided to go to war with Afghanistan. England wanted to strengthen Russia's ties with

---

[38] Hopkirk, Peter. «The Great Game: The Struggle for Empire in Central Asia.» Kodansha International, 1992.

Afghanistan and wanted to keep Afghanistan under its influence.

The war took place in the military territories of England and Afghanistan. England has used her hands in both liquid and dry regions, supporting the advice of her powerful movements in that place between generations. Afghanistan, on the other hand, mobilized its fighting men and fought with England and its co-produced arms.

The result of the war was the reason for the resurgence of the army on the part of Afghanistan. In May 1880, a number of international powers, which lost Afghanistan's independence, met in May 1880.

During the reign of Abdurahman Khan (1880-1901), Afghanistan gained internal political stability and a centralized state structure. His policy was aimed at conciliating Britain and strengthening control over the tribes within the country. Abdurahman Khan carried out large-scale reforms to create a centralized state. These reforms were aimed at strengthening control over tribes and various groups within the country. The centralized state structure played an important role in ensuring the internal stability of Afghanistan[39]. Abdurrahman Khan's policy was aimed at limiting British and Russian influence. He signed treaties of peace and friendship with Britain and tried to keep the country independent in its internal affairs. Abdurrahman Khan's policy was one of Afghanistan's attempts to get out of semi-colonialism[40].

This war took place in the military territories of England and Afghanistan. England has used her hands in both liquid and dry regions, supporting the advice of her powerful movements in that place between generations. Afghanistan, on the other hand, mobilized its fighting men and fought with England and its co-produced arms. The result of the war was the reason for the revival of the army by Afghanistan. In May 1880, a number of international powers, which lost Afghanistan's independence, met in May 1880. They faced unique challenges, including Afghanistan's geography and changing land use.

---

[39] Kakar, M. Hassan. «Afghanistan: The Soviet Invasion and the Afghan Response, 1979-1982.» University of California Press, 1995.
[40] Gregorian, Vartan. «The Emergence of Modern Afghanistan: Politics of Reform and Modernization, 1880-1946.» Stanford University Press, 1969.

With the Afghan government and population at odds, they were looking at a grim alternative. As a result of this war, Afghanistan strengthened its support for the Afghan Khanate and its chances of achieving independence.

The establishment of a protectorate in British Afghanistan was an important historical event that took place in the late 19th and early 20th centuries. Britain strengthened its influence in Afghanistan during the two Anglo-Afghan wars of 1839-1842 and 1878-1880. As a result of these wars, Afghanistan lost its independence and Afghanistan became an important geographical location for development. Later, in 1880, with the advent of Abdur Rahman Khan's rule in Afghanistan, Britain tried to strengthen its influence in Afghanistan. Abdurrahman Khan established Afghanistan's military relations with other countries, and these relations helped strengthen British economic and political influence in Afghanistan.

Later, in the late 19th and early 20th centuries, Britain established a "protectorate" regime in Afghanistan. In this regime, Afghanistan formally lost its independence, but was de facto under the influence of the British government. British influence in Afghanistan's political and economic spheres was achieved through, for example, the creation of legal and executive instruments, advice to the Afghan government and the establishment of political agreements. Britain also helped build infrastructure projects in Afghanistan, such as road and rail networks, parks, water sources, and communication facilities. These were steps aimed at strengthening the influence of the British government in Afghanistan, establishing mutual production networks and regulating the political and economic life of Afghanistan.

Although British rule in Afghanistan changed over the course of the 19th and 20th centuries, it mainly had the following stages:

1. Protectorate (1878-1919): As a result of the second Anglo-Afghan war, which ended in 1878, Afghanistan was forced to comply with several conditions. Britain increased its influence in the political and economic spheres of Afghanistan. During this period, Afghanistan formally lost its independence, but was de facto under the influence of the British government. The British

strengthened their political influence by providing advice to the Afghan government, determining the rule of law and the executive of Afghanistan.

2. Re-supporting the country's independence (1919-1929): In 1919, England officially recognized the independence of Afghanistan. The British drafted documents to support Afghanistan's independence and government features. They helped to advise the Afghan government and make the country's political decisions.

3. Afghan Municipal Forces and National Government (1929-1973): In 1929, the British withdrew from Afghanistan, and at the same time, Afghanistan gained independence. During this period, the urban forces of Afghanistan came into conflict with each other, and national governments were established in the country. The national government of Afghanistan attempted to achieve independence in its political and economic affairs.

4. Soviet occupation (1979-1989): In 1979, the Soviet Union deployed its soldiers to Afghanistan and occupied the country. During this period,

Afghanistan was ruled by the Soviet government, and the country experienced major political and economic changes.

The British rule was important in the history of Afghanistan and played a major role in the political, economic and social development of the country. At the beginning of the 20th century, efforts aimed at restoring the national sovereignty of Afghanistan intensified. In 1919, during the Third Anglo-Afghan War, Afghanistan gained its independence.

3.3. Independence and the third war

Afghan troops led by Amanullah Khan fought against the British forces and succeeded. As a result of the war, the Treaty of Rawalpindi was signed in 1919, according to which Afghanistan gained complete independence and received the right to independently determine its foreign policy[41]. Amanullah Khan implemented large-scale reforms after independence. These reforms were aimed at modernization of the country, development of the education system and strengthening of the economy. His policy was aimed at turning Afghanistan into a modern country[42].

The third Anglo-Afghan war took place in the years 1919-1921 and was called the "War of the Mountain and the Living". The main reason for this war is the British desire to strengthen its influence in Afghanistan and to define the country's political, economic and cultural life. In flight, the national groups fighting for

---

[41] Saikal, Amin. «Modern Afghanistan: A History of Struggle and Survival.» I.B. Tauris, 2004.

[42] Edwards, David B. «Before Taliban: Genealogies of the Afghan Jihad.» University of California Press, 2002.

Afghanistan's independence are known to be protected from neighboring foreign governments and countries that exert enormous political and economic influence on the country. In particular, Bolshevist Russia and Bashkortostan turned a blind eye to independence in Afghanistan. In this war, the British Afghan government tried to protect its political and economic interests and tried to increase its influence in Afghanistan.

As a result, the resistance between the Afghan government and the national warring factions strengthened their hand to read the war between Britain and Afghanistan. After this war, the Anglo-Afghan Treaty of Friendship was signed in 1921, and the independence of Afghanistan was restored. As a result of the independence and consolidation of the government of Afghanistan, the country faced changes in its political and economic sphere and embarked on the path of national development.

The struggle against the British is an important indicator in the history of Afghanistan, which includes wars and conflicts with other countries. These types of struggles depend on many factors, including:

1. Colonial and Protectorate Policy: The British Empire tried to get closer to the territories of Afghanistan, to contain it and to destroy the independent government. This policy led to step-by-step wars learned by the Afghan people and government.

2. Religious and Hymn Statements: As a Muslim country in Afghanistan, religious and hymn values were important in confronting the British. As a result, religious motives were established in showing an alternative to the struggle against the British.

3. National identity: The people of Afghanistan fought to preserve their national identity and fought against the captured military forces. National declarations, adat-independent values, music, literature and the national idea were the basis for many studies to preserve this identity.

4. Independence and Sovereignty: Afghanistan fought to maintain its independence and sovereignty, and particularly in the face of the British, it tried to protect its territories and restore its independent government.

These and other reasons caused the struggle between the people of Afghanistan and the government against the British. These struggles included many wars and disturbances, but they were of great importance for strengthening the national spirit of Afghanistan and maintaining its independence and sovereignty.

The restoration of Afghanistan's independence was the result of a continuous and multi-layered process. This process can be seen in the following steps:

1. Anglo-Afghan War (1878-1880): This war was of great importance to support the independence of Afghanistan. A war with other countries to settle the dispute between the British and the Russians represented an attempt by Afghanistan to maintain its independence.

2. Pan-Islamism and Bashkortostan (1890-1900s): During this period, Russia worked on the side of Bashkortostan to support the independence of Afghanistan. The national war in Afghanistan can be very important in terms of distribution itself, because it is a national layer against alternative Russia.

3. 1919-1929: During this period, the process of re-supporting the independence of Afghanistan took place. The British government recognized the independence of Afghanistan and in 1919 the Afghan National Government restored the independence of Afghanistan and in 1921 the Anglo-Afghan Treaty of Friendship was signed.

4. Soviet occupation (1979-1989): In 1979, the Soviet Union deployed its soldiers to Afghanistan and occupied the country. In this process, the Afghan government and national struggle groups waged a war against the Soviet occupiers. The war ended in 1989 with the withdrawal of Soviet troops.

5. Soviet External Insurgency and the Najibullah Era: Soviet external insurgency and developments during the 1980s helped strengthen Afghanistan's independence. In 1992, Najibullah's government fell, and the Afghan people adopted a new political and economic vision to support Afghanistan's independence again.

The restoration of Afghanistan's independence is a continuous process, and its history has various processes, wars and political changes. National movements, national governments, public uprisings, and persecution by the international community also played a major role in the restoration of independence.

CONCLUSION

At the end of the 1860s, critical comments on this matter became stronger, as a result of the announcement of the "Reform Decree" and the consequences of its implementation, Turks and Muslims lost their dominant position in their country. The "Uzins" were able to make good use of such a situation that arose in the society and left the enemies behind in every field. "New Ottomans" (1865) included Turkish intellectuals, journalists, teachers, and officials, who were supporters of the constitutional system. In the 70s of the 19th century, Turkey became a colony of foreign countries, the country was drawn into the world capitalist market. 137 foreign banks were opened here. Turkey was one of the last places in the world in terms of industrial production. In 1876 (May 30), the leader of the liberal group, Midhat Pasha, made a palace coup together with the new Ottomans. Sultan Abdulhamidl sat on the throne. He approved the draft constitution produced by Midhat Poshho and he solemnly announced it on December 23, 1876. But at the beginning of 1877, the sultan dismissed Midhat Pasha from the prime ministership. He repressed the "New Ottomans". Parliament was dissolved and autocracy was restored. This period in the history of Turkey was called the "period of oppression". Democratic change was banned, terror and insecurity increased in the country. Turkey's defeat in the Russo-Turkish War of 1877-1878 put an end to its dominance in the Balkans.

Involvement of Iranian agriculture in the field of commodity relations has led to increased state pressure on farmers. The development of commodity-money relations and the growth of money taxes led to the increase of usury. The increase in the commoditization of agriculture and the establishment of private ownership of land systematically reduced the peasants' share of the harvest and increased taxes, which led to the ruin and impoverishment of the peasantry. In the late 19th century, mass expulsion of peasants from the land and deprivation of the right to "perpetual rent" contributed to this. Devastated peasants fled to the cities, where they joined bankrupt artisans and small manufacturers. The city became the center of popular protest. Although there were no major popular uprisings in Iran in the second half of the 19th century after the Babi revolts of 1848-1852, popular discontent erupted in spontaneous riots in Tehran and other parts of the country. The influx of foreign capital into Iran affected not only the state of the nation. This exacerbated all the contradictions of the Qajar state with the traditionally weak influence of the central government on the tribes and khans. The economic subjugation of Iran to the interests of foreign capital, its transformation into a dependent state of England and Russia, violated the economic conditions for the creation of a national industry in the country. The unlimited power of the Qajars created insurmountable obstacles for the emergence of entrepreneurship in Iran and slowed down the formation of a national industrial bourgeoisie.

The Second Anglo-Afghan War was a turning point in the development of the people of Afghanistan. It is true that the Afghan sovereign State retained independence in internal affairs, Afghanistan had customs autonomy and knew neither capitulation regime nor foreign loans. But its foreign policy came under British control, it became a "forbidden" country, cut off from the rest of the world. Using Indian merchants as comprador intermediaries, British capital occupied the Afghan market. The subsidies paid to Abdurahman by the British government determined the financial dependence of the Afghan government on England. The last decades of the 19th century and the beginning of the 20th century saw a significant increase in commodity-money relations, and a capitalist structure began to take shape in the feudal Afghan economy. Domestic and foreign trade increased, agricultural specialization expanded, and the city's population increased. With the help of foreign engineers, Abdurrahman created a number of small state-owned enterprises and weapons production workshops. These new processes in the Afghan economy were the beginning of the emergence of a common Afghan market and the emergence of a national (Afghan) commercial bourgeoisie, which entered into competition with Indian and Tajik merchants.

Afghan landowners and merchants were interested in strengthening the central government. Abdurrahman significantly increased his army. The army became the main weapon of the ruling classes against the rebel khans and tribal leaders, as well as against the peasants and oppressed peoples. By the end of the century, Abdurrahman managed to break the resistance of the big feudal lords and deprive them of political independence. A unified monetary system, unified measures of weight and length were introduced. Of course, the weakness of the bourgeois elements of Afghan society, the preservation of feudal-patriarchal relations between nomadic and semi-nomadic Afghan tribes limited the possibilities of centralization of the country, but nevertheless, by the end of the 19th century. Afghanistan, for example, was a more centralized and powerful country than neighboring Iran.

The process of semi-colonization of Turkey, Iran and Afghanistan developed under the economic, political and military influence of foreign countries in the 19th and early 20th centuries. The struggle for independence of these countries was aimed at restoring their national sovereignty. The Ottoman Empire and the Republic of Turkey, the period of Iran and Reza Shah Pahlavi, and the independence movement of Afghanistan are vivid examples of these processes. The struggle for the restoration of national sovereignty and the creation of a modern state occupies an important place in the modern history of these countries.

References:

1. Анаркулова Д.М. Общественно-политическая деятельность Мальком-хана. – Душанбе, 1984.

2. Avery, Peter. «Modern Iran.» Praeger Publishers, 1965.

3. Amanat, Abbas. «Iran: A Modern History.» Yale University Press, 2017.

4. Abrahamian, Ervand. «A History of Modern Iran.» Cambridge University Press, 2008.

5. Баумгартен В. Поездка по Восточной Персии Л.-Гв. Волынского полка Поручика Баумгартена в 1894 году. (географически-торговое исследование). – СПб., 1896.

6. Campos, Michelle U. «Ottoman Brothers: Muslims, Christians, and Jews in Early Twentieth-Century Palestine». Stanford University Press, 2011.

7. Cronin, Stephanie. «The Army and the Creation of the Pahlavi State in Iran, 1921-1926.» I.B. Tauris, 1997.

8. Dupree, Louis. «Afghanistan.» Princeton University Press, 1973.

9. Edwards, David B. «Before Taliban: Genealogies of the Afghan Jihad.» University of California Press, 2002.

10. Faroqhi, Suraiya. «The Ottoman Empire and the World Around It». Cambridge University Press, 2004.

11. Gregorian, Vartan. «The Emergence of Modern Afghanistan: Politics of Reform and Modernization, 1880-1946.» Stanford University Press, 1969.

12. Hopkirk, Peter. «The Great Game: The Struggle for Empire in Central Asia.» Kodansha International, 1992.

13. Inalcik, Halil. «The Ottoman Empire: The Classical Age 1300-1600». Phoenix Press, 2000.

14. Kinross, Lord. «Atatürk: The Rebirth of a Nation.» Weidenfeld & Nicolson, 1964.

15. Kakar, M. Hassan. «Afghanistan: The Soviet Invasion and the Afghan Response, 1979-1982.» University of California Press, 1995.

16. McMeekin, Sean. «The Ottoman Endgame: War, Revolution, and the Making of the Modern Middle East, 1908-1923». Penguin Press, 2015.

17. Millyyer A.F. Osmanskaya imperiya v nachale XX veka. M. 1974.

18. Novaya istoriya stran zarubejnoy Azii i Afriki M., Nauka. 1971.

19. Noelle-Karimi, Christine. «State and Tribe in Nineteenth-Century Afghanistan: The Reign of Amir Dost Muhammad Khan (1826-1863).» Routledge, 1997.

20. Olson, Robert. «The Siege of Mosul and Ottoman-Persian Relations, 1718-1743: A Study of Rebellion in the Capital and War in the Provinces of the Ottoman Empire.» Indiana University, 1975.

21. Saikal, Amin. «Modern Afghanistan: A History of Struggle and Survival.» I.B. Tauris, 2004.

22. Yangi tarix T., «O'qiluvchi» 1969 y.

23. Yapp, Malcolm E. «The Near East Since the First World War: A History to 1995.» Longman, 1996.

24. Zürcher, Erik J. «Turkey: A Modern History.» I.B. Tauris, 2004.

SAPARBAEVA AZIZA

Saparbayeva Aziza is the daughter of Asror. Urganch State University, Faculty of Socio-Economic Sciences, 4rd stage student of history education. Navoi state scholarship winner.

The author of more than 40 articles and 5 books, a member of 10 international organizations, a graduate of more than 20 international courses, the holder of a badge for international services of the Kazakhstan "Qo'shqanot" creative association, a participant in the international project of the Oxford&UrSU Amudarya Project, the founder of the Student Academy project, "Zukko kitobxon" June 2022 winner of the 3rd place contest, 2nd place winner of the district stage of the Young Reader republican contest, winner and participant of more than 30 international and republican competitions, participant of more than 20 international and republican scientific-practical conferences, graduate of the Shine Girls Academy.